WILLESDEN JUNCTION TO RICHMOND

Vic Mitchell and Keith Smith

MP Middleton Press

First published March 1996

ISBN 1 873793 71 5

© Middleton Press 1996

Design - Deborah Goodridge

Published by Middleton Press
        Easebourne Lane
        Midhurst
        West Sussex
        GU29 9AZ
        Tel: 01730 813169
        Fax: 01730 812601

Printed & bound by Biddles Ltd,
        Guildford and Kings Lynn

CONTENTS

28	Acton Central
21	Acton Wells Junction
74	Bollo Lane Junction
83	Gunnersbury
35	Hammersmith & Chiswick Branch
70	Kew
72	Kew Bridge
68	Kew East Junction
102	Kew Gardens
14	Old Oak Junction
111	Richmond
44	South Acton
63	South Acton Junction
8	Willesden High Level Junction
1	Willesden Junction (High Level)

MAPS AND DIAGRAMS

I	Route diagram
II	Central area enlargement 1955
III	Willesden Junction area 6" 1912
IV	Acton Central 25" 1915
V	Central area 6" 1912
VI	Hammersmith Branch 6" 1873
VII	Acton Coal Depot 25" 1915
VIII	Hammersmith & Chiswick 25" 1894
IX	South Acton 25" 1915
X	Kew Bridge area 25" 1935
XI	Bollo Lane Junction 25" 1915
XII	Gunnersbury 25" 1885
XIII	Gunnersbury 25" 1894
XIV	Gunnersbury 25" 1935
XV	Kew Gardens 25" 1886
XVI	Richmond Gas Works 25" 1895
XVII	Richmond 25" 1893

ACKNOWLEDGEMENTS

We are very appreciative of the help received from the photographic contributors mentioned in the captions and also for the assistance given by P.G.Barnes, D,Clayton, G.Croughton, J.B.Horne, G.A.Jacobs, N.Langridge, D.Lovett (North London Railways Corporate Affairs), Mr D.& Dr.S.Salter, G.T.V.Stacey, D.Trevor Rowe and our ever helpful wives.

GEOGRAPHICAL SETTING

Willesden Junction is over 100ft above sea level and is situated on London Clay. The line drops steadily to Gunnersbury, traversing Brickearth in the Acton area. The final section of the route is on the flood plain gravels of the Thames Valley.

The maps are to the scale of 25 ins to 1 mile, unless otherwise shown.

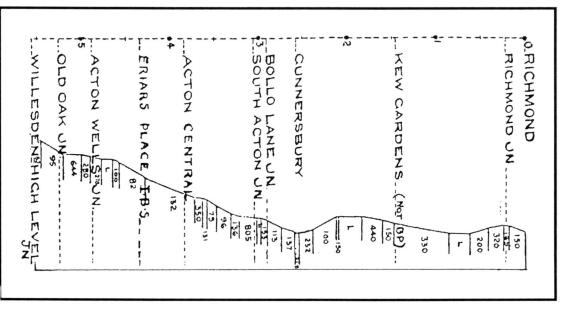

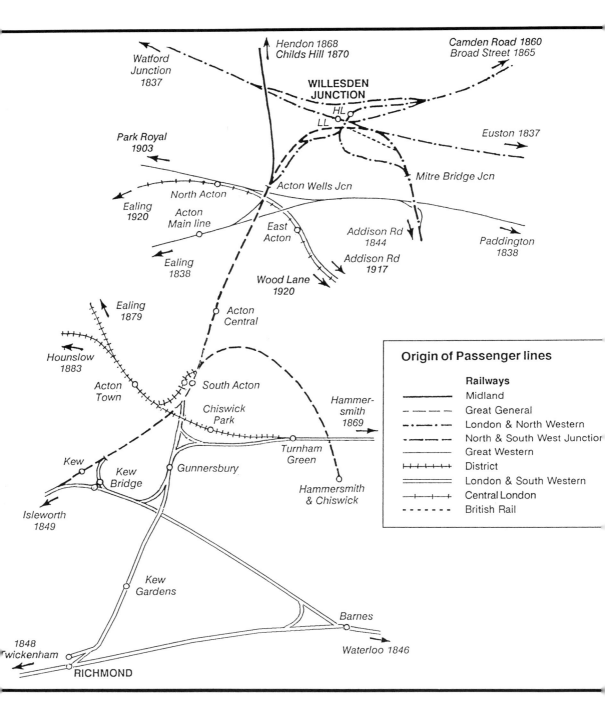

I. Route diagram showing origin of the lines, dates of associated routes and last used names of stations.

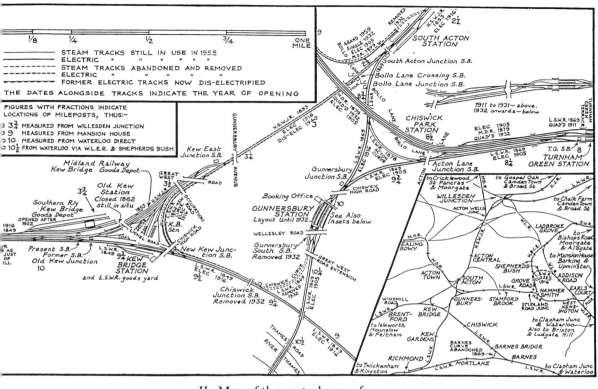

II. Map of the central area of
the route in 1955. (J.C.Gillham)

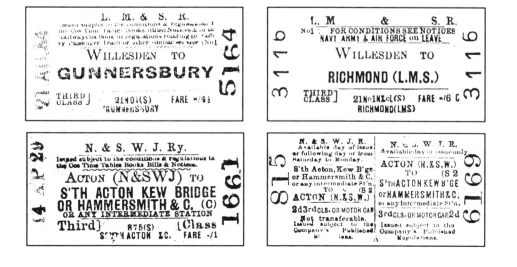

HISTORICAL BACKGROUND

An Act of Parliament for the construction of the North & South Western Junction Railway was obtained in 1851, the line being leased jointly by the London & **North** Western Railway and the London **& South Western Railway.** The purpose of the route was to link together these two expanding systems, primarily for the transfer of goods traffic, this commencing on 15th February 1853. It was worked initially by the LSWR.

Nearly four miles long, the railway ran from a London-facing junction near Willesden to one facing away from London near Kew. Passenger services commenced on 1st August 1853 but these were operated by the North London Railway. The opening years of the other lines in the area are shown on map I and the dates of the opening of the stations on the route are given in the captions.

NLR trains were extended from Kew to Twickenham from 20th May 1858 but this involved reversals at Kew and Barnes. (They were worked south of Kew by the LSWR). Curves were added to form triangular junctions at these places on 1st February 1862, thus allowing direct running.

These facilities were of value for only a short time, as a direct line to Richmond from a junction south of Acton was opened by the LSWR on 1st January 1869. NLR trains then used this route and continued to Kingston. The Act for this three mile long line was passed in 1864. It also gave the LSWR consent to build a line from Gunnersbury to Kensington (Addison Road, now Olympia) via Turnham Green, Hammersmith (Grove Road) and Shepherds Bush (see inset on map II). This route, which also opened on 1st January 1869, was in the shape of a question mark seen in a mirror and was certainly of questionable value. The straight part was used by the District Railway for its Richmond trains from 1st June 1877 and the curve through Shepherds Bush was abandoned on 5th June 1916.

The Midland Railway opened a link between its main line and the NSWJR on 1st October 1868 and operated several short-lived passenger services. One was to Earls Court and used a curve laid in 1878 to form a triangular junction north of Gunnersbury.

The NSWJR had new lessees from 1871 - the LNWR, NLR and the Midland jointly, but the NLR ran most of the passenger services.

The different origins of the two parts of the route have continued to be evident over the years. Willesden Junction to South Acton became part of the London Midland and Scottish Railway in 1923 and the London Midland Region of British Railways in 1948. The southern part of the route was incorporated into the Southern Railway and the Southern Region of BR in the same years. The District Railway became part of London Transport on 1st July 1933. Most of the Gunnersbury - Hammersmith section was transferred from BR to LT on 23rd January 1950.

Hammersmith & Chiswick Branch

The NSWJR opened this 1½ mile long branch on 1st May 1857 to goods and 8th April 1858 to passengers. The latter service ceased on 1st January 1917 and the former on 3rd May 1965. The line was abandoned on 1st January 1966.

Electrification

District Railway trains to Richmond were electrically operated from 1st August 1905, those to Ealing having started exactly one month earlier.

North London Line electric trains commenced running to Kew Bridge and Richmond on 1st October 1916. (The NLR had been operated by the LNWR since 1st February 1909 and was taken over in 1922).

Conductor rails between South Acton and Kew Bridge were soon lifted following cessation of passenger services on 12th September 1940.

PASSENGER SERVICES

The NSWJR owned only one locomotive, most services being operated by a number of other companies. Different railways also worked over the LSWR section of the route. All these companies are considered below.

North London Railway

From the opening of the NSWJR to passengers, the NLR ran four trains per day between Hampstead Road (where Primrose Hill Station is now) and Kew, using the LNWR main line east of Willesden. From 1st June to 31st October 1854, some of these journeys were extended to Windsor. From 20th May 1858 the trains, now eight per day, ran on to Twickenham, involving reversals at Kew and at Barnes; three of them started from Fenchurch Street. From 1st July 1863 nine or ten weekday trains were terminating at Kingston. From 2nd January 1860, NLR trains worked via Gospel Oak (known as Kentish Town until 1st February 1867), and from 1st November 1865 most originated at the company's new terminus at Broad Street, running at a basic 30 minute interval as far as Kew, with nine continuing to Kingston. With the completion of the direct line to Richmond on 1st January 1869, alternate trains terminated there and at Kew Bridge. The interval was reduced to 15 minutes in 1912, still with alternating termination points.

London & South Western Railway

The LSWR did not work scheduled services over the NSWJR. The initial timetable for their 1869 part of the route showed trains from London (Waterloo and Ludgate Hill) running to Richmond via Kensington Addison Road, Shepherds Bush, and Turnham Green. A frequent service was operated for many years but a steady decline in this century resulted in cessation on 3rd June 1916.

A Clapham Junction to Hounslow service was provided from 1901 to 1909. This used the same circuitous route to Gunnersbury where it turned west to Isleworth.

Metropolitan Railway

This company operated a Moorgate - Richmond service from 1877 to 1894. It was extended to Aldgate from 1894 to 1907.

Great Western Railway

For part of 1870, a Paddington-Richmond service ran via Notting Hill (now Ladbrooke Grove) and Turnham Green. The same route was used from 1894 to 1906 by the Metropolitan Railway for a service starting in the City. It was cut back to start at Notting Hill from 1907 to 1910, during which period it was operated again by the GWR.

A rural connection between Willesden Junction and Southall (on the main line west of Ealing) was provided from 1888 to 1912. In its latter years, this was worked by a railmotor.

Midland Railway

In 1875, the MR put on a service from the City (Moorgate Street) to Richmond via Childs Hill but it was cut back to that place in 1876 and then discontinued.

Undeterred, the MR tried a St.Pancras to Earls Court timetable in 1878-80. This ran via Childs Hill, Acton, and Turnham Green.

Their final use of the route for local passenger trains was between 1894 and 1902, when a link between Childs Hill and Gunnersbury was provided.

District Railway

This company extended its operation from Hammersmith to Richmond in 1877, using almost entirely LSWR rails. It ran to Ealing from 1879, using its own branch from Turnham Green.

The branch to South Acton had a passenger service from Hounslow from 13th June 1905 until 14th February 1932. From that date until closure on 1st March 1959 there was only a shuttle service from Acton Town.

The electric era

District Line trains have originated from various stations, out as far as Upminster. Train frequency to Richmond has been as high as six per hour, but not necessarily at regular intervals.

North London Line trains from Broad Street ran at 30 minute intervals outside the peak hours, passengers for Kew Bridge having to change at Acton into a branch train. In 1922 the weekday interval was reduced to 15 minutes but the Kew Bridge connection remained at 30.

For most of the 1940s the interval was 20 minutes and has varied between 15 and 30 subsequently. Most trains have originated at North Woolwich instead of Broad Street since May 1985, although there was much curtailment due to various engineering works in the early 1990s, east of Willesden Junction.

Hammersmith & Chiswick Branch

For most of the early years a basic hourly service was provided from Acton, with extras in the peak hours. After the opening of South Acton in 1880, a half-hourly timetable was operated as branch trains could then terminate there. On Sundays there were two early morning trips and then a "church interval" until about noon when the normal frequency was resumed.

A similar pattern was employed until closure, although in the final years there were no trains on Sunday mornings as the railmotor was used then between South Acton and Kew Bridge. This type of train was introduced in 1909.

August 1916

August 1916

WATERLOO, KENSINGTON, GUNNERSBURY, RICHMOND, and TWICKENHAM.—L. & S. W.

Miles	Down.	mrn	mrn	mrn	mrn	mrn	mrn		mrn	mrn	mrn		mrn	mrn	mrn		aft	aft	aft	aft		aft
	Week Days.																Runs to Staines Junction, see page 136.					
	Waterloo ....dep.			6 37		7 55			9 10		1012			1130				1 12		2 15		
1¼	Vauxhall			6 42		8 0			9 14		1017			1137				1 17		2 20		
2¾	Queen's Road §			6 46		8 4			9 18		1020			1140				1 20		2 23		
—	**Clapham** Junction ....dep.	5 40	6 35		7 40		8 50			9 53			1050		1150				1 53			
4	Battersea	5 43	6 38	6 50	7 43	8 7	8 53		9 22	9 56	1024		1053	1143	1153			1 23	1 56	2 26		2 53
4¾	Chelsea and Fulham	5 46	6 41	6 53	7 46	8 10	8 56		9 25	9 59	1027		1056	1147	1156			1 26	1 59	2 29		2 56
5½	West Brompton ....[381	5 48	6 43	6 55	7 48	8 12	8 58		9 27	10 1	1029		1058	1149	1158			1 28	2 1	2 31		2 58
6½	**Kensington** (Addison Road)	5 53	6 49	7 4	7 52	8 17	9 3		9 32	10 6	1033		11 3	1154	12 5			1 32	2 6	2 35		3 3
7¼	Shepherd's Bush *	5 56	6 52	7 7	7 55	8 20	9 6		9 35	10 9	1036		11 6	1157	12 8			1 35	2 9	2 38		3 6
7¾	**Hammersmith** (Grove Road)	5 59	6 55	7 10	7 58	8 23	9 9		9 38	1012	1039		11 9	12 0	1211			1 38	2 12	2 41		3 9
8¼	Ravenscourt Park	6 1	6 57	7 13	8 1	8 26	9 11		9 41	1014	1042		1111	12 3	1214			1 41	2 14	2 44		3 12
9	Turnham Green †	6 4	7 0	7 16	8 5	8 29	9 14		9 44	1017	1045		1114	12 6	1217			1 44	2 17	2 47		3 15
10	Gunnersbury	6 8	7 4	7 20	8 11	8 33	9 18		9 48	1022	1049		1118	1210	1221			1 49	2 22	2 51		3 19
11	Kew Gardens			7 23		8 37			9 52		1053			1214				1 53		2 55		3 23
12½	**Richmond** (New) ....arr.			7 27		8 41			9 56		1057			1218				1 57		2 59		3 27
14½	**136Twickenham** ....arr.			7 39		9 2			1013		1116			1240				2b23		3 20		3 39
—	Gunnersbury ....dep.	6 8	7 4		8 11		9 18			1022			1118		1221		1 15		2 22			3 35
10¾	Kew Bridge **383**	6 11	7 7		8 14		9 21			1025			1121		1224		1 18		2 25			3 38
11¾	**Brentford** ‡	6 14	7 10		8 17		9 24			1028			1124		1227		1 21		2 29			3 41
13¼	Isleworth and Spring Grove.	6 17	7 13		8 20		9 27			1031			1128		1230		1 24		2 33			3 44
14	**Hounslow and Whitton**	6 22	7 18		8 25		9 31			1036			1133		1235		1 27		2 37			3 48
16½	**Twickenham 136** .....arr.	6 28	7 23		8 30		9 36			1041			1138		1240				2 42			3 54

Down.	aft	aft	aft	aft		aft	aft	aft	aft	aft	aft		aft	aft	aft	aft	aft	aft
Week Days—*Continued.*																		
Waterloo ....dep.	3 28		4 30				5 33	6 30			7 40			8 42		1020		1140
Vauxhall	3 33		4 35				5 38	6 35			7 45			8 47		1025		1145
Queen's Road §	3 37		4 39				5 41	6 38			7 48			8 51		1029		1148
Clapham Junction ...dep.		3 50		4 43		5 36			6 44	7 40			8 45		9 50		1117	
Battersea	3 41	3 53	4 42	4 46		5 39	5 45	6 41	6 47	7 43	7 53		8 48	8 54	9 53	1033	1120	1152
Chelsea and Fulham	3 44	3 56	4 45	4 49		5 42	5 48	6 44	6 50	7 46	7 56		8 51	8 57	9 56	1036	1123	1155
West Brompton ....[381	3 46	3 58	4 47	4 51		5 44	5 50	6 46	6 52	7 48	7 58		8 53	8 59	9 58	1038	1125	1157
Kensington (Addison Road)	3 50	4 5	4 51	4 56		5 48	5 54	6 50	6 56	7 52	8 3		8 57	9 3	10 4	1042	1130	12 2
Shepherd's Bush *	3 53	4 8	4 54	5 0		5 51	5 57	6 54	6 59	7 55	8 5		9 0	9 6	10 7	1045	1133	12 5
Hammersmith (Grove Road)	3 56	4 11	4 57	5 3		5 54	6 0	6 57	7 2	7 58	8 8		9 3	9 10	1010	1048	1136	12 8
Ravenscourt Park	3 59	4 14	4 59	5 5		5 56	6 3	7 0	7 4	8 0	8 11		9 5	9 13	1012	1051	1138	1211
Turnham Green †	4 2	4 17	5 2	5 8		5 59	6 6	7 3	7 7	8 3	8 14		9 8	9 16	1015	1054	1141	1214
Gunnersbury	4 5	4 21	5 14	5 11		6 4	6 10	7 8	7 11	8 7	8 18		9 13	9 20	1019	1058	1145	1218
Kew Gardens	4 9			5 15			6 14	7 12			8 22			9 23		11 2		1222
Richmond (New) ....arr.	4 13			5 19			6 18	7 16			8 26			9 27		11 6		1227
136Twickenham ....arr.	4 31			5 33			6 28	7 36			8 40			9 39		1116		1247
Gunnersbury ....dep.		4 21	5 14			6 4			7 11	8 7			9 13		1019		1145	
Kew Bridge **383**		4 24	5 18			6 7			7 14	8 10			9 17		1022		1148	
Brentford ‡		4 27	5 22			6 10			7 17	8 13			9 20		1025		1151	
Isleworth and Spring Grove.		4 31	5 26			6 13			7 20	8 16			9 23		1028		1154	
Hounslow and Whitton		4 36	5 31			6 17			7 24	8 21			9 28		1033		1157	
Twickenham 136 .....arr.		4 41	5 36			6 22			7 29	8 26			9 33		1038			

Down.	mrn	mrn	mrn	a	mrn	aft	a	aft	a	aft	a	aft	a	aft	a	aft	aft	aft	a	aft	aft	aft
Sundays.																						
Waterloo ....dep.	7 35	9 0		1025			1230		2 25		3 30		5 30		6 30				8 30		1020	
Vauxhall	7 40	9 5		1030			1235		2 30		3 35		5 35		6 35				8 35		1025	
Queen's Road §	7 43	9 8		1033			1238		2 33		3 38		5 38		6 38				8 38		1028	
Clapham Junction ....dep.																						
Battersea	7 46	9 12		1036			1241		2 36		3 41		5 41		6 41				8 41		1032	
Chelsea and Fulham	7 49	9 15		1039			1244		2 39		3 44		5 44		6 44				8 44		1035	
West Brompton ....[381	7 51	9 17		1041			1246		2 41		3 46		5 46		6 46				8 46		1037	
Kensington (Addison Road)	7 55	9 21		1046			1250		2 46		3 50		5 50		6 50			8 25	8 50		1041	
Shepherd's Bush *	7 58	9 24		1049			1253		2 49		3 53		5 53		6 53			8 28	8 53		1045	
Hammersmith (Grove Road)	8 2	9 27		1052			1256		2 52		3 56		5 56		6 56			8 31	8 56		1049	
Ravenscourt Park	8 5	9 30		1055			1259		2 55		3 59		5 59		6 59			8 33	8 59		1052	
Turnham Green †	8 8	9 33		1058			1 2		2 58		4 2		6 2		7 2			8 36	9 2		1055	
Gunnersbury	8 12	9 37		11 2			1 6		3 3		4 6		6 6		7 6			8 40	9 6		1059	1125
Kew Gardens	8 16	9 41		11 6			1 10		3 7		4 10		6 10		7 10			8 44	9 10		11 2	1128
Richmond (New) ....arr.	8 20	9 45		1110			1 14		3 11		4 14		6 14		7 14			8 48	9 14		11 6	1133
138Twickenham ....arr.	8 38	10 1		1117			1 21		3 21		4 21		6 21		7 21			9 16	9 21		1115	1140
Gunnersbury ....dep.	8 26	9 44	1023	1110	1139	1252	1 53	2 40	3 30	4 20	4 39	5 39	6 10	6 30	7 34	8 11	8 26	8 53	10 0	1025	1128	
Kew Bridge **383**	8 29	9 47	1026	1113	1142	1255	1 56	2 43	3 33	4 23	4 42	5 42	6 13	6 33	7 37	8 14	8 29	8 56	10 3	1028	1131	
Brentford ‡	8 32	9 50	1029	1116	1145	1258	1 59	2 46	3 36	4 26	4 45	5 45	6 16	6 36	7 40	8 17	8 32	8 59	10 6	1031	1134	
Isleworth and Spring Grove.	8 35	9 53	1032	1119	1148	1 1	2 2	2 49	3 39	4 29	4 48	5 48	6 19	6 39	7 43	8 20	8 35	9 2	10 9	1034	1137	
Hounslow and Whitton	8 40	9 56	1037	1124	1151	1 6	2 5	2 54	3 42	4 32	4 53	5 51	6 24	6 44	7 48	8 23	8 40	9 7	1012	1039	1140	
Twickenham 138 .....arr.	8 45		1042	1129		1 11		2 59			4 58		6 29		7 53		8 45	9 12		1044		

a Run to Kingston, see page 139. *b* Arrives at 2 11 aft. on Saturdays.

* About ¼ mile to the Metropolitan Station. † Turnham Green (Bedford Park). ‡ ¼ mile to Great Western Station.

§ Station for East Battersea and North West Clapham.

July 1906

CHILD'S HILL, STONEBRIDGE PARK, and GUNNERSBURY.—Midland.

Fares from Child's Hill. 1 cl.	3 cl.	Return 1 cl.	Return 3 cl.	Down.	mrn	mrn	mrn	mrn	mrn	aft		aft	aft	aft	aft	aft	aft		
				London (St. Pancras) **449** ....dep.				9 10			Saturdays only.	3 15	4 40		6 27	7 25	8 55		
				Child's Hill and Cricklewood.......dep.	7 20	8 2	8 43	10 9	1157	2 47		3 40	5 7	6 15	7 10	8 0	9 30		
0 3	0 1½	0 6	0 3	Dudding Hill, for Willesden & Neasden..	7 24	8 6	8 47	1014	12 1	2 51		3 44	5 11	6 19	7 14	8 5	9 34		
0 5	0 2½	0 8	0 5	**Stonebridge Park** *	7 27	8 9	8 50	1019	12 4	2 55		3 47	5 14	6 22	7 17	8 9	9 37		
0 8	0 4	1 1	0 7	Acton	7 34	8 15	8 56	1026	1210	3 2		3 53	5 20	6 28	7 23	8 16	9 43		
0 9	0 4½	1 2	0 7	South Acton	7 36	8 17	8 58	1028	1212	3 4		3 55	5 22	6 30		8 18	9 45		
0 9	0 5	1 2	0 9	**Gunnersbury 335, 343, 118, 333**..arr.	7 38	8 19	9 2	1032	1217	3 6		3 58	5 25	6 33	7 25	8 21	9 47		

Fares 1 cl.	3 cl.	Return 1 cl.	Return 3 cl.	Up.	mrn	mrn	mrn	mrn	aft	aft		aft	aft	aft	aft	aft	aft		
				Gunnersbury ....dep.	8 12	8 43	9 28	1043	1259	3 12	Saturdays only.	4 10	5 35	6 59	7 35	8 40	1035		
0 3	0 1	0 5	0 2	South Acton	8 14	8 45	9 31	1046	1 2	3 15		4 13	5 38	7 3		8 43	1038		
0 3	0 1	0 5	0 2	Acton	8 16	8 48	9 34	1048	1 4	3 17		4 15	5 41	7 5	7 38	8 45	1041		
0 6	0 3	0 9	0 5	**Stonebridge Park** *	8 22	8 54	9 41	1054	1 10	3 23		4 21	5 49	7 11	7 44	8 52	1049		
0 9	0 3½	1 2	0 7	Dudding Hill, for Willesden & Neasden..	8 26	8 58	9 45	1058	1 14	3 27		4 26	5 53	7 16		8 57	1054		
0 9	0 5	1 2	0 9	**Child's Hill and Cricklewood**.......arr.	8 30	9 3	9 51	11 2	1 20	3 31		4 31	5 57	7 20	7 50	9 2	11 0		
1 0	0 6	1 6	0 10	London (St. Pancras) **451** ....arr.			1015			4 0							1145		

* Station for West Willesden and Harlesden.

January 1901

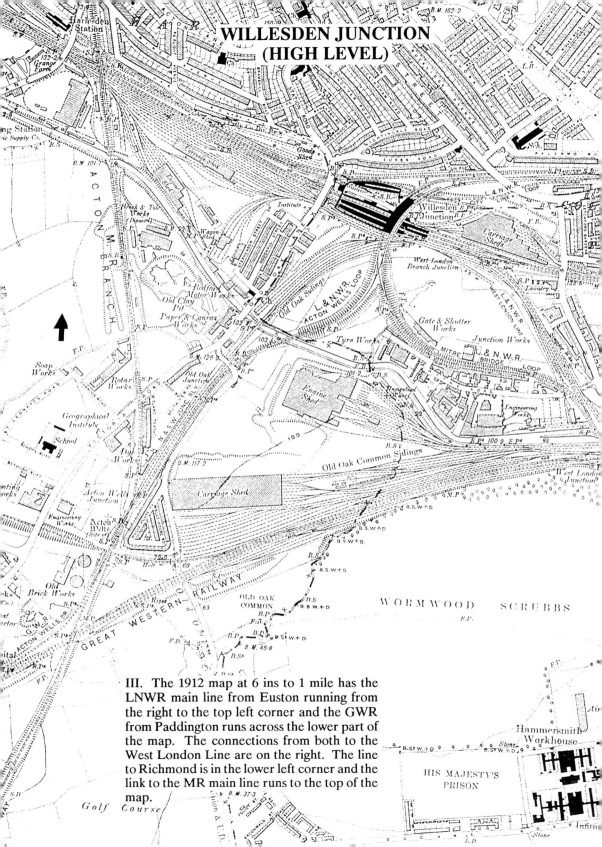

WILLESDEN JUNCTION
(HIGH LEVEL)

III. The 1912 map at 6 ins to 1 mile has the LNWR main line from Euston running from the right to the top left corner and the GWR from Paddington runs across the lower part of the map. The connections from both to the West London Line are on the right. The line to Richmond is in the lower left corner and the link to the MR main line runs to the top of the map.

1. A northward view shows a 2-4-2T terminating a local train at platform 10 prior to 1923. On the right are the four flights of steps leading down to the main line platforms. The first station on the main line was in use from 1842 to 1866. The name of the box is Willesden High Level Junction. (Lens of Sutton)

2. This and the next photograph show the condition of the Richmond line platform in October 1953. The derelict platform had been used mainly by LMS electric trains to Kensington (Addison Road) until their withdrawal on 20th October 1940. (H.C.Casserley)

3. The signals by Willesden High Level Junction signal box allowed trains from either platform to join the Kensington or Richmond routes. The rambling gaslit station was one of the least popular junctions in the London area and was partially rebuilt in 1957. (H.C.Casserley)

4. A Richmond-bound train approaches the new building in 1961, after platform 11 and its associated conductor rails had been removed. The main line platforms were closed on 3rd December 1962 and the remaining platforms renumbered subsequently. (Pamlin Prints)

5. A westward view from the High Level in November 1979 includes the footbridges leading to the 1912 Low Level station. These platforms serve Bakerloo and Euston-Watford Junction local electric trains. A train loaded with cars is on the Hampstead-Wembley freight line. The main entrance to the station is in the building in front of the middle cooling tower; the building on the left serves as an entrance during peak hours. (J.C.Gillham)

6. A class 313 unit arrives on 4th October 1989 during the first week of operation of these units, although the plan had been to introduce them in May. The fourth rails were removed in the early 1970s since which time the return current has passed through the running rails. (F.Hornby)

7. HST no. 43014 from Edinburgh is bound for Waterloo on 7th July 1995, the third day of operation of this Eurostar connecting service which is restricted to the carriage of inter-national passengers. Through Eurostar trains to Europe from Scotland on this track were planned for the summer of 1996. (M.Turvey)

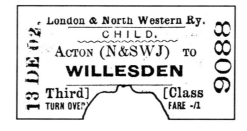

WILLESDEN HIGH LEVEL JUNCTION

8. A class 501 unit leaves the High Level station on 25th November 1979 and passes over the then still new replacement spans over the main lines. The bridge for up trains is on the left. The next two pictures were taken on the same day. (J.C.Gillham)

9. The signal box is at the south end of the bridge and largely obscures the ex-LNWR Old Oak sidings. The Richmond trains pass over the bow-string bridge visible to the left of the box. (J.C.Gillham)

10. Taken from almost the same viewpoint as the previous picture, this shows the Kensington lines on the left and a train departing for Richmond. The bow-string structure carries the line over the Grand Union Canal and appears in several of the following photographs. (J.C.Gillham)

11. Looking south from platform 5 on 9th August 1994, we see the bridges that replaced the old ones in the Spring of 1976, the junction box and the rear of a new Networker class 456 unit coupled to a translator van. They were about to run onto the West London Line and were hauled by two class 47 locomotives. (V.Mitchell)

12. A westward view under the bridges seen in the previous picture shows the junction (foreground) betwen the electrified goods line to Brent Sidings and the line to Acton Wells.

It was taken from the opposite side of the train shown in the next picture. The main line to the north is on the right. (V.Mitchell)

13. The back of the box and the end of Old Oak sidings are viewed from the 14.20 Brighton to Manchester Piccadilly on 2nd November 1991.

Three reversible running tracks had recently been provided at this point. (V.Mitchell)

OLD OAK JUNCTION

14. Two 3-car units have just passed over the junction on their way from Richmond to Broad Street on 20th July 1958. High Level Junction Box is in the centre distance. The coaches had manually operated sliding doors at the ends of each saloon. (A.E.Bennett)

15. Class Q1 0-6-0 no. 33013 is about to pass over the Grand Union Canal on 26th September 1959, while working freight from the London Midland Region to the Southern. The wall appears in the next picture. (T.Wright)

16. Southbound with inter-regional freight on 18th July 1964 is no. D5513. Class 30 later became 31. The road bridge from which this and the next picture was taken gave access to the Western Region Old Oak Common Depot. The box was in use from 1892 until 6th November 1977. (T.Wright)

17. A train from Richmond rattles over the junction on the same day. On the right is the original 1853 route which was mostly at ground level to the junction with the LNWR. (T.Wright)

18. Looking north from the same bridge on 15th September 1992, we see new track on the old route and the 14.20 Brighton to Manchester running southwards on its northerly journey behind no. 47817. Until 27th October 1990 such trains reached the line to Reading via West London Junction (see right of map III) but land there was required for the Eurostar Depot. They have subsequently used the BR connection shown at the top of map I (and seen in picture no. 13) to reach Reading. The HST on the left is working empty from Old Oak Common Depot to Euston prior to operating a Holyhead service. The loop in the background was signalled for passenger trains, all the new lines being bidirectional. (J.N.Faulkner)

19. Four tracks ran parallel to Acton Wells Junction following the elimination of the junction at Old Oak. This picture was taken on 19th September 1995 from the same position as no. 17. The pantograph on the roof of no. 313004 would be used on 25kV AC wires between Camden Road and Acton Central from 2nd June 1996. (T.Wright)

20. Another southward view from the same bridge on the same day. Acton Wells Box is near the rear of the train which probably originated at Southampton Docks and is hauled by no. 47339. (T.Wright)

ACTON WELLS JUNCTION

21. This and the next two photographs were taken on 4th May 1957. Ex-LSWR class H16 no. 30516 was one of five 4-6-2Ts designed by Urie specifically for freight work between the MR Brent Yard, the LNWR Willesden Yard and the LSWR's new marshalling yard at Feltham, which was its destination that day. (R.C.Riley)

22. The 1877 connection to the GWR is on the right as two 3-car units from Richmond approach the junction. The LMS built two batches of compartment stock (in 1927 and 1933), all third class, to supplement or replace some of the original units. (R.C.Riley)

23. Two 3-car Oerlikon units glide past the junction box and the 35 mph speed limit board. There were about eighty such units and also four of similar design built by Siemens. (R.C.Riley)

24. Looking north, with the signal box behind us, we see class 37 no. D6916 with oil tankers from Ripple Lane (Barking) bound for Staines West. Standing on the 1868 MR connection is class 47 no. D1672 with a short freight train from Brent on 12th December 1970. (J.N.Faulkner)

25. A 2EPB unit runs towards Richmond on 17th July 1985 and passes over the Paddington - Ealing main line; the connection to this is on the left. It has just passed over the Paddington - High Wycombe route and the Central Line. Old Oak Common carriage shed is to the right of the houses. (R.Palmer)

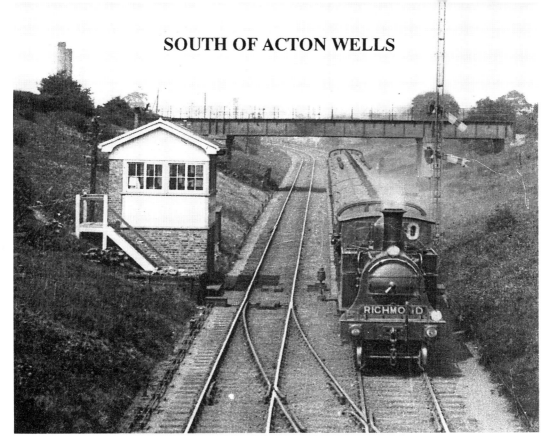

26. A NLR 4-4-0T passes Friars Walk box in about 1902. This and the bridge, which appears to simply link two fields, shows in the lower left corner of map III. The box closed in February 1935. (K.Nunn/LCGB)

27. BR class 5 4-6-0 no. 73155 climbs the 1 in 132 gradient from Acton Central to Acton Wells Junction with the Saturdays only 10.29 Poole-Bradford train on 23rd July 1966. A housing estate has since replaced the prefabs on the right. (J.N.Faulkner)

ACTON CENTRAL

IV. The 1915 edition includes a loop north of the station and a bay platform at its south end. Local trains to Hammersmith & Chiswick used this and there was provision for the locomotive to run round its short train clear of the main line. Note that the High Street tramway converges to interlaced track under the railway bridge.

28. The station opened with the commencement of passenger services on the route and was completely rebuilt in 1876. This frontage faced Churchfield Road and was at a right angle to the track. The suffix "Central" was added on 1st November 1925. Trains never ran direct to the last four places listed. (Lens of Sutton)

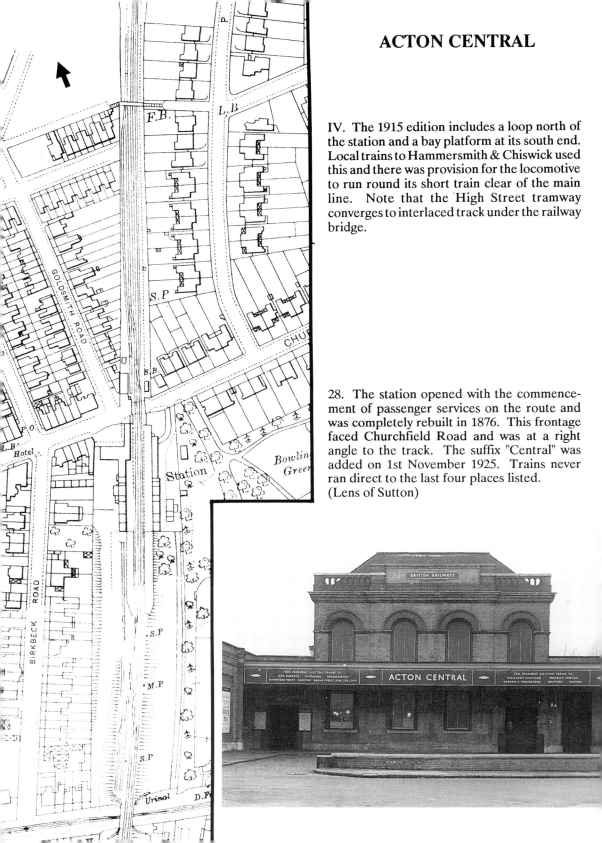

29. A northward view in the 1950s includes the white sighting board for the up starting signal. Part of the loop shunt signal is also silhouetted against it. The bridge carries a public footpath. (Lens of Sutton)

30. The 12.0 noon football special from Tunbridge Wells West passes over the siding facing points on its way to Wembley Stadium behind U class 2-6-0 no. 31904 on 19th June 1953. Goods sidings usually had trailing points. The former bay line was used for freight until 1st March 1965. (N.W.Sprinks)

31. The loop was electrified for use by trains working a shuttle service to Kew Bridge. Running to Feltham Yard on 1st March 1958 is class G16 4-8-0T no. 30493, one of a batch of four built in 1921 for hump shunting there. The second wagon is for coke. (J.N.Faulkner)

32. The down side canopy was extensively damaged by fire on 17th February 1981, this being the scene on 14th June following. There is evidence of one stanchion having failed at an earlier date. (R.Palmer)

33. A telephoto view from the footbridge on 27th February 1983 features a fine example of NLR coaching signals on a lattice post. A Broad Street bound class 501 approaches the site of the loop. (R.Palmer)

34. A September 1995 photograph shows the main building in commercial use and the down side devoid of shelter. The unburnt part of the canopy was retained for many years but subsequently passengers were expected to wait in the open and snow could gather on the subway steps. (M.J.Stretton)

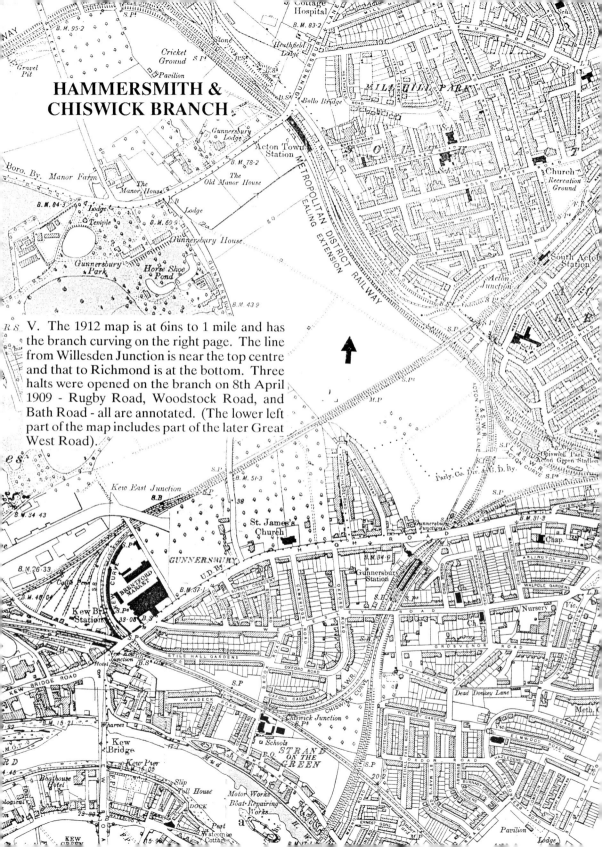

HAMMERSMITH & CHISWICK BRANCH

V. The 1912 map is at 6ins to 1 mile and has the branch curving on the right page. The line from Willesden Junction is near the top centre and that to Richmond is at the bottom. Three halts were opened on the branch on 8th April 1909 - Rugby Road, Woodstock Road, and Bath Road - all are annotated. (The lower left part of the map includes part of the later Great West Road).

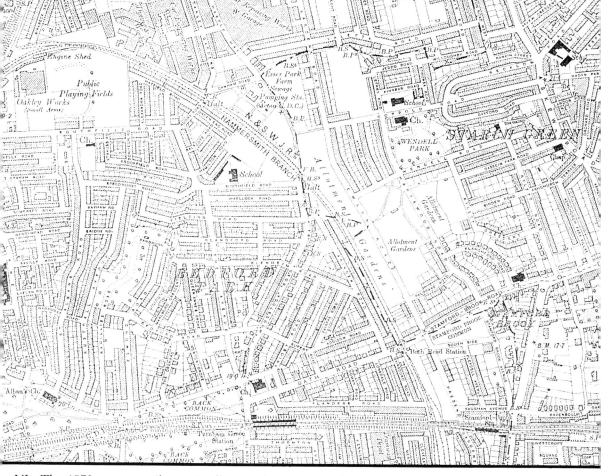

VI. The 1873 survey at 6ins to 1 mile reveals the rural nature of the district at that time, also that sufficient land was taken for double track. The line opened for goods in 1857 and for passengers in 1858. An "Engine House" is shown near the terminus. The NSWJR's only locomotive was kept here until 1860. One or two coaches were uncoupled from down NLR trains near the junction, sometimes unofficially while still on the move. This gave rise to rumours of slip coach operation. NLR locomotives worked the branch after 1860 and through working of coaches ceased in 1865.

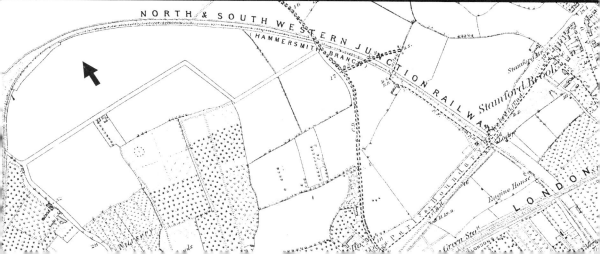

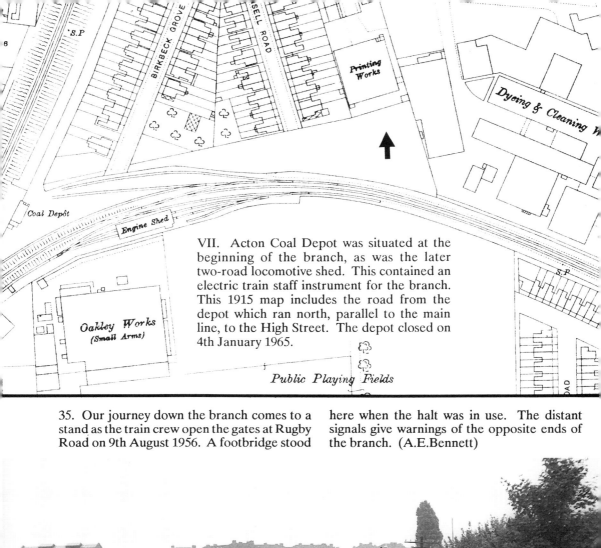

VII. Acton Coal Depot was situated at the beginning of the branch, as was the later two-road locomotive shed. This contained an electric train staff instrument for the branch. This 1915 map includes the road from the depot which ran north, parallel to the main line, to the High Street. The depot closed on 4th January 1965.

35. Our journey down the branch comes to a stand as the train crew open the gates at Rugby Road on 9th August 1956. A footbridge stood here when the halt was in use. The distant signals give warnings of the opposite ends of the branch. (A.E.Bennett)

36. A LNWR steam railcar worked most services on the branch from 1909 until traffic ceased on the last day of 1916. One such unit is seen from the footbridge at Woodstock Road Halt. (Lens of Sutton)

37. The site of Woodstock Road Halt is seen in this southward view from September 1956. It seems that the branch was not on the itinerary of the weed killing train that year. (A.E.Bennett)

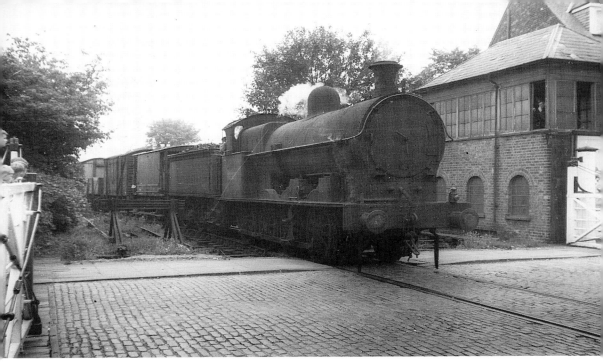

38.   Ex-LMS 0-8-0 no. 49277 crosses Bath Road, the site of the final halt for railmotors. By the time that this photograph was taken in August 1956, the signal box functioned as a ground frame and was manned only during shunting. (A.E.Bennett)

39. The box was recorded on 24th July 1965; all traffic had ceased on 3rd May previous. A single lever ground frame is on the left. (T.Wright)

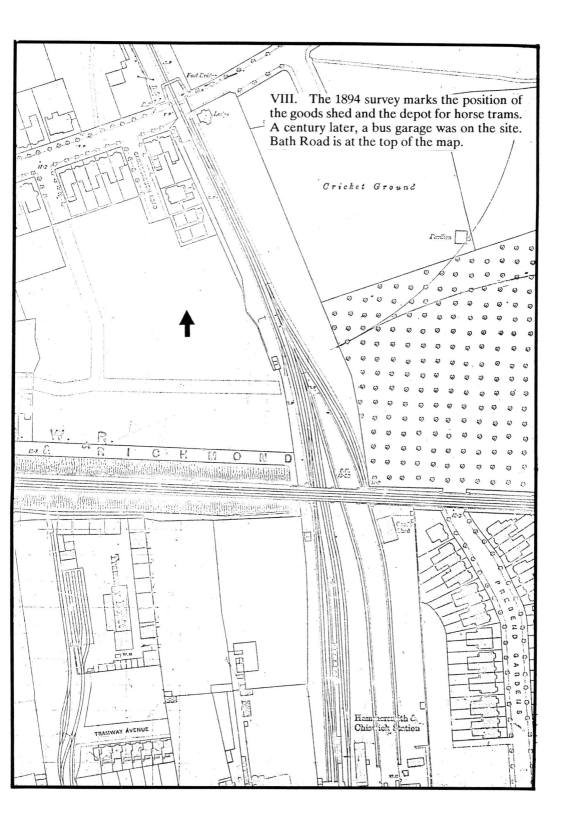

VIII. The 1894 survey marks the position of the goods shed and the depot for horse trams. A century later, a bus garage was on the site. Bath Road is at the top of the map.

Cricket Ground

W. P. R I C H M O N D

TRAMWAY AVENUE

Hammersmith & Chiswick Station

40. The station had been just "Hammersmith" until 1st July 1880 when "&Chiswick" was added. It was near neither but was of value to those needing to travel to and from Chiswick High Road. The ramp on the platform was presumably for the benefit of railmotor passengers. Stratton Gentry & Co. were coal merchants. (R.M.Casserley coll.)

41. The northern part of the goods yard was recorded on 9th August 1956, coal being the predominant traffic. The use of solid fuel declined rapidly in the 1950s following disastrous smogs and consequent legislation. (A.E.Bennett)

42. Further south, the long yard was crossed by the District and Piccadilly Lines; the west end of Stamford Brook station is on the left. Also visible is general goods traffic and the 5-ton crane. A RCTS railtour visited the branch on 10th November 1956. (J.J.Smith)

43. The tour ran in awful weather and did not enter the platform. BR class 4 2-6-4T no. 80065 has hauled the train from South Acton and is about to run round through the last Summer's weeds. (S.C.Nash)

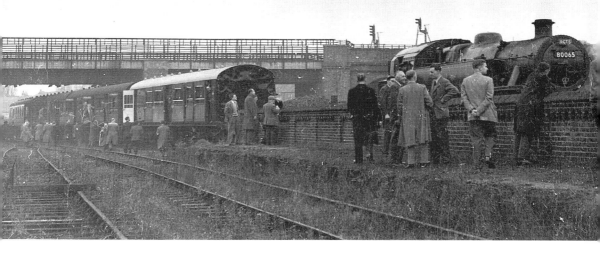

SOUTH ACTON

IX.   The top right corner of this 1915 map almost joins the left side of map VII. Near the lower border is Acton Junction where the Richmond and Kew Bridge routes diverge. To the left is the District Railway branch from Acton Town, then double track. Note the bay platform and run round for H&C branch trains. The NSWJR station opened nearly 30 years after the main line, on 1st January 1880. The signal box (S.B.) in the centre of the map is "District Junction" and was opened on 15th May 1899. It also controlled the H&C junction from 1st September 1909. Prior to this date the junction had been worked by Hammersmith Junction box, which had been situated in the vee of the junction. The bridge over Acton Lane replaced a level crossing in 1874. The points of District Junction were clipped out of use in 1915 and were removed in 1930, along with the signal box. The signal box shown on the District platform was added in 1905 to work a facing crossover (just off the map) which allowed branch trains into the only platform. The signalman also sold tickets from 1913 until the box was abolished in 1932.

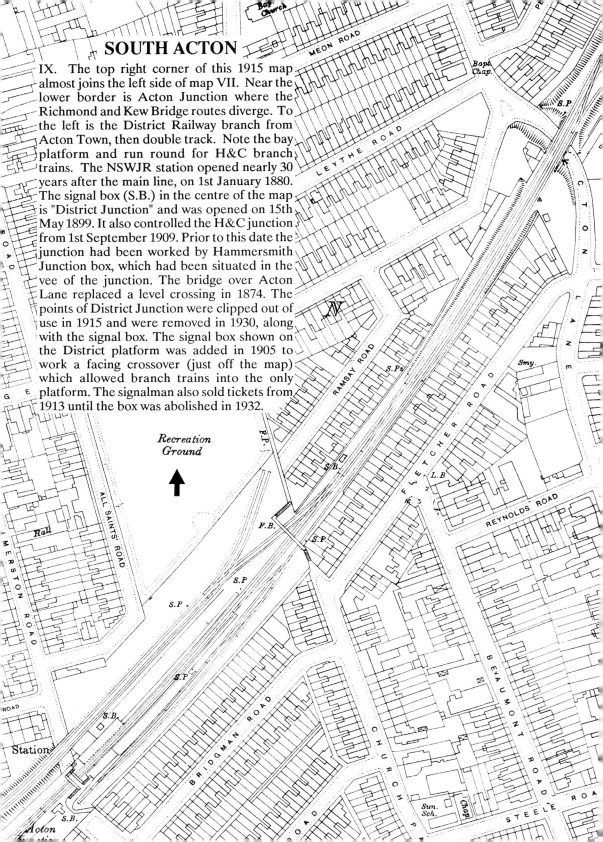

44. The LNWR's power station at Stonebridge Park had four turbo-alternators producing current at 11000 volts, 25 cycles to feed the sub-stations. This is the one in Acton Lane, north of South Acton station, where rotary convertors generated DC at 660 volts for the conductor rails. (British Rail)

45. A Willesden - Feltham freight transfer plods through slowly on 13th June 1945 behind SR class 0395 0-6-0 no. 3163, built by Neilsons in 1883. Coupled to it are two new 0-6-0STs (nos. 75293 and 75294) for the War Department, probably en route to the Longmoor Military Railway. (S.C.Nash)

46. The H & C branch curved away beyond the north end of South Acton station; its signal is clear for a branch train to arrive. Acton Coal Yard is in the background and Oerlikon stock is bound for Broad Street on the left. (A.E.Bennett)

47. Long passenger trains were seen only on special occasions. This is the 1.18pm football excursion from Orpington to Wembley Stadium on 19th June 1953, headed by class N1 2-6-0 no. 31879. (N.W.Sprinks)

48. The RCTS railtour on 10th November 1956, seen in picture nos. 42 and 43, was worked from Willesden Junction by no. 42118, a LMR class 4 2-6-4T. No. 80065 coupled on to the other end of the train for the branch tour, ran to Richmond and returned the members to Willesden Junction. (H.C.Casserley)

49. The MR had two goods depots in Kensington which were accessed via the District Line. Empty coal wagons are being brought back from them by ex-MR 0-6-0T no. 47226, classified 3F. The Acton Town single car is on the right on 1st March 1958. (J.N.Faulkner)

50. One of the GEC all-compartment units departs north on 24th July 1958 displaying the then obligatory oil lamp in addition to the inbuilt electric one. (J.C.Gillham)

51. A southward view from the Church Path footbridge in July 1958 includes the connection to the branch, its bay platform and run round loop. On the left is the milk dock. The District station is in the centre background. (J.C.Gillham)

52. South Acton Junction is in the distance in this southward view and the LT District Line station is on the right. The left distant arm concerned drivers of goods trains bound for Kensington. (Lens of Sutton)

53. Single track came into use in 1899 and was used mainly by construction trains in connection with the extension of the District line. The link to the NSWJR does not seem to have ever carried a regular service although it was doubled just prior to electrification in 1905. A peculiarity is the bridge in the foreground which passes over the end of a cul-de-sac. The bridges on the branch were removed in January 1964. (Lens of Sutton)

54. One of two specially modified motor coaches, each with two driving compartments, was used to provide the service to Acton Town about every ten minutes. It was an early example of one-man operation. The vehicles had a curious swaying motion when travelling. This 1953 view includes a bomb site. (N.W.Sprinks)

55. The District Railway services commenced on 13th June 1905; full passenger facilities being provided here. The two nearest doorways were for ladies and gentlemen. The ticket office was at the far end of the building. (R.M.Casserley coll.)

56. One car fitted neatly under the canopy which protected the well illuminated clock. The place had an incongruous air with the paradox of a rural branch line station being served by an urban type of train. (T.Wright)

57. Two entrances were provided, securely separated by unclimbable railings, although you could walk round the end of the wall. The closure notice is up for the end of services to Acton Town on 2nd March 1959. The last train ran on 28th February prior. (J.J.Smith)

58. The end of the line in both senses. Two class 501 units depart for Broad Street and pass under the footbridge for Church Path which once spanned five tracks. (J.J.Smith)

59. Milk tankers stand at the former bay platform on a gloomy day in 1963. The diagonal fencing on the up platform could be found on widely scattered LMS stations. (Pamlin Prints)

60. No. 47240 roars north with freight on 5th March 1983. The semaphore signalling lasted a few more months but the wooden platforms continued in use until 1986. The LT Chiswick Works for bus overhaul is in the background. (R.Palmer)

61. No. 25199 hauls ballast for track work on the line on 23rd October 1983. There is a new approach to the up platform and a minimal shelter on the down side. (R.Palmer)

62. A photograph from September 1995 shows the addition of a fretted valence by the booking office (open mornings only), a new vaulted shelter on the down platform and modern track. There is a crossover in the distance. (M.J.Stretton)

SOUTH ACTON JUNCTION

63. Here the route divides, left for Gunnersbury and right for Kew Bridge. A view from the booking office entrance shows an LSWR Adams 4-4-0 with MR clerestory coaches. (Lens of Sutton)

64. The driver of class G2 0-8-0 no. 49277 is ready to hand the token to the signalman on 9th August 1956. This was for the single line H&C branch. We last saw this locomotive in picture no. 38. (A.E.Bennett)

65. Empties from Kensington clatter round the curve on 24th July 1958 behind class 3F 0-6-0T no. 47433. The conductor rails were removed from the Kew Bridge line early in World War II. (J.C.Gillham)

➤

66. The extensive use of timber is noteworthy; apart from the rails and bridge foundations most things are wooden in this 1963 view. The box closed on 23rd August 1970 after which date the points were controlled from Bollo Lane Junction Box, which had been Bollo Lane Crossing Box until that time. (Pamlin Prints)

➤

67. A class 313 unit accelerates towards Bollo Lane Junction Box (left) on 19th September 1995, as a Piccadilly Line train traverses the background. The LT works in the background was subsequently demolished. Our journey to Richmond continues at picture no. 80. (T.Wright)

KEW EAST JUNCTION

X. The junction is top right on this 1935 map and lower left on map V. The former LSWR route from Barnes to Isleworth runs from right to left. The original Kew station is to the left of Lionel Road bridge. The sidings within the triangle were originally used by the MR. Kew Bridge Goods Depot (left) was an SR creation, the earlier LSWR yard being south of the main line. Freight traffic ceased on 3rd April 1967. The private siding for the stoneworks branches from a line known as "Rhubarb Siding". Kew Bridge station (lower centre) was opened on 1st February 1862 as "Kew" and renamed in December 1868. (Kew is south of the river). The crane shown was of 5-ton capacity. Kew Curve Box was situated on that curve in LSWR days.

Potomac (Fish Pond)

Boat House

Factory (Potato Crisps)

Engineering Works

Playing Field

Engineering Works

Crane

Stone Works

W.M.

Lodge

Kew Bridge Goods Depôt

S.P.

S.P.

S.P.

Coal Depot

BM.29·83

Old Kew Junction S.P.

S.B.

DRAGON LANE

30

Filter Beds

Filter Beds

Filter Beds

W.M.

35

Kew Bridge Water Works

34 (Met. Water Board)

Filter Bed

Reservoir

Wells

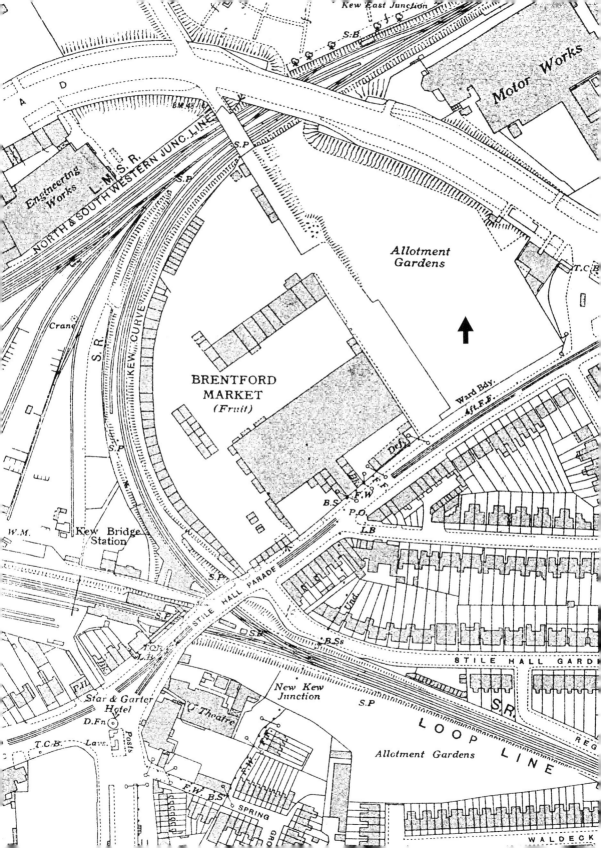

Kew East Junction

S.B.

Motor Works

A D

BM

S.P

Engineering Works

L. M. S. R.

NORTH & SOUTH WESTERN JUNC. LINE

S.B.

Allotment Gardens

T.C.B

Crane

S.R.

KEW CURVE

BRENTFORD MARKET
(Fruit)

Ward Bdy.
4ft. F.E.

T.C.B

S.P

Def.

F.F

B.S.

F.W.

P.O.

W.M.

Kew Bridge Station

L.B.

S.P

STILE HALL PARADE

Und.

STILE HALL GARD

S.P

S.P

T.C.B.

L.B.

B.Ss

New Kew Junction

S.R.

F Ph

S.P

L O O P   L I N E

REG

Star & Garter Hotel

C Theatre

D.Fn.

Posts

Allotment Gardens

T.C.B.

Laws.

F.W.

B.S

F.W. B.S

SPRING

WALDECK

68. Ex-LNER class J6 0-6-0 no. 64266 eases an assortment of wagons from Feltham across the junction on 30th March 1957. There were four parallel lines for some distance beyond the Great West Road bridge at that time. Note the small signal arm for permissive working. This allowed goods trains to queue up on the curve to Old Kew Junction. (S.C.Nash)

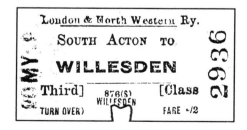

London & North Western Ry.

SOUTH ACTON TO

WILLESDEN

Third] [Class

876(S)
WILLESDEN

TURN OVER) FARE -/2

2936

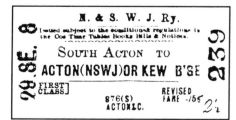

N. & S. W. J. Ry.

Issued subject to the conditions & regulations in the Coo Time Tables Books Bills & Notices.

SOUTH ACTON TO

ACTON(NSWJ)OR KEW B'SE

FIRST
CLASS]

876(S)
ACTON1C.

REVISED
FARE -/55

239

L. ... & ... S. R.
Issued subject to the conditions & regulations in the Co's Time Tables books &c. No Luggage allowed except ... Railway ... Passenger Train or other ... service
ACTON (CENTRAL) TO
KEW BRIDGE
(L)
THIRD CLASS   875(S)   FARE -/1½
KEW BRIDGE
1547

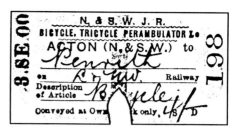

N. & S.W. J. R.
BICYCLE, TRICYCLE PERAMBULATOR &c
ACTON (N. & S.W.) to
Penrith
on   R. & W.   Railway
Description of Article   Bicycle
Conveyed at Owner's risk only. 4/S/D
3. SE. 00
198

69. The small shunt signal had been replaced by a distant arm by the time the "Kentish Katabasis" was recorded on 14th January 1984. A narrow bodied Hastings line DEMU was used by the Lea Valley Railway Club on a railtour from Watford to various branches in Kent. We are looking from the Great West Road bridge; the bridge in the distance is for Gunnersbury Avenue. (R.Palmer)

KEW

70. Originally the southernmost of the two NSWJR stations, it was simply "Kew" and closed on 1st February 1862, although the weekly train from Windsor to the Metro-politan Cattle Market continued to use it for a time. This is a 1920 view towards Kew East Junction. (K.Nunn/LCGB)

71. Looking towards Old Kew Junction in April 1953, we see the original station three years before its demolition. Part of the platforms remained until 1968. Both tracks on this part of the route between the two junctions were subject to permissive working. (R.K.Kirkland)

KEW BRIDGE

72. One of the LMS 2-6-2T class 3Ps fitted with condensing apparatus creeps towards New Kew Junction with a milk train on the 10-chain curve. Electric trains from Broad Street terminating here usually used the opposite platform which was connected to the former LSWR up platform by a tunnel under Lionel Road. (Lens of Sutton)

73. After an interval of about 30 years, steam reappeared on the same curve for some pre-Christmas weekend trips from Kensington Olympia. BR class 4 2-6-4T no. 80079 is working the circular tour via Willesden and Clapham Junctions on 17th December 1994. The NSWJR had its own booking office here until 1918. (R.Palmer)

The LSWR part of the station and photographs of the junction appear in the companion album *Kingston and Hounslow Loops.*
(Out of print 1996)

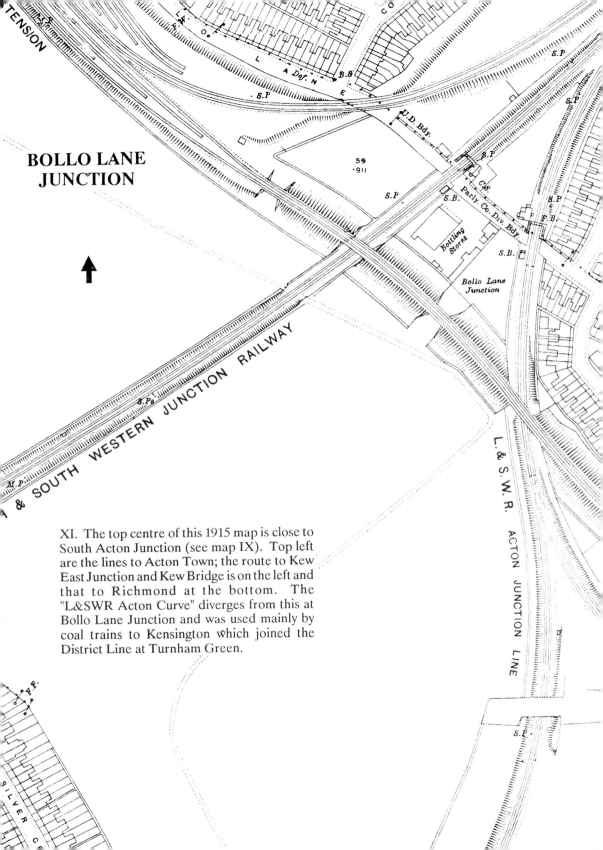

BOLLO LANE JUNCTION

XI. The top centre of this 1915 map is close to South Acton Junction (see map IX). Top left are the lines to Acton Town; the route to Kew East Junction and Kew Bridge is on the left and that to Richmond at the bottom. The "L&SWR Acton Curve" diverges from this at Bollo Lane Junction and was used mainly by coal trains to Kensington which joined the District Line at Turnham Green.

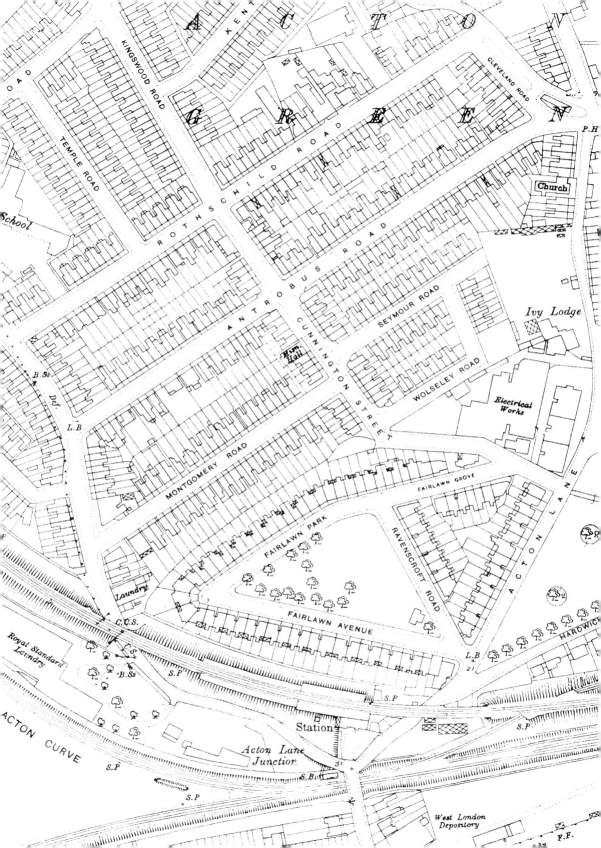

74. This (and the next picture) was taken from the footbridge at Bollo Lane level crossing on 24th August 1957. The bracket of the down junction signals and South Acton station appear in this view. (J.C.Gillham)

75. A Richmond - bound Oerlikon unit passes under the bridge carrying the District and Piccadilly Lines and approaches the junction where Kensington-bound coal trains turned left. (J.C.Gillham)

76. The gatewheel seen in the previous picture was removed when the extension to the box was built to house the barrier controls. The map shows another box close by on the adjacent level crossing. This closed on 21st January 1974 when barriers came into use on both crossings. Seen in 1995, the box then also controlled South Acton Junction and the barriers at Acton Central by CCTV. (M.J.Stretton)

77. Freight trains ran to High Street Kensington until the depot there closed on 25th November 1963. The first MR coal train had arrived there on 1st March 1878. Acton Lane Junction box was to the right of the camera and was in use until 13th October 1968, although the Acton Curve had been out of use since 11th September 1965, officially. Ex-LMS "Jinty" class 3F 0-6-0T no. 47435 was photographed on 27th July 1955. (J.C.Gillham)

78. Looking east from the other side of Acton Lane bridge a few minutes later, we see the flyunder built in 1911 for up District trains. These trains had used the southern pair of tracks between Turnham Green and Hammersmith until 1932. The northern pair were used by the LSWR until 1916 and then lay derelict until 1932. From that year, Piccadilly Line trains used the middle pair and District the outside two. The freight is about to pass under a footbridge and then under the southern two tracks to join the eastbound Piccadilly line. (J.C.Gillham)

79. Having passed through Turnham Green (the driver's prayer) on the Piccadilly Line (lower right), freight trains then passed onto a fifth track (second from the left) on which they could wait if necessary for a gap between eastbound District trains. Traffic continued to the ex-MR West Kensington depot until 14th July 1965. This eastward view of the fifth line in July 1963 includes a speeding westbound Piccadilly train. The reason for this complicated route was that the gradient on the 1911 line was steep for steam trains. Map II (top right) clarifies the evolution. (J.C.Gillham)

80. A District Line train destined for Richmond approaches Gunnersbury and is seen from Chiswick High Road at the southern apex of the triangle on 7th March 1964. The tracks from South Acton (left) once had a six-car gap in the conductor rails to avoid trains connecting the LMR and LT power systems. Single units suffered a prolonged current loss when coasting over the break; it was gloomy at night. (J.N.Faulkner)

81. The box was named East Box until 29th May 1932 and was photographed in September 1976. It closed on 26th March 1980, after which date the junction was controlled from Richmond. London Transport's main scientific laboratory is also visible. (J.Scrace)

82. Gunnersbury Junction was photographed from the north end of the down platform on 6th September 1995 as a class 313 unit leaves for Stratford. Trains terminated there instead of Woolwich from 29th May 1994 until 29th October 1995, during construction work for the Jubilee Line. Milepost 10 shows the distance from Waterloo via Shepherds Bush. The bridge carries Chiswick High Road. (M.Turvey)

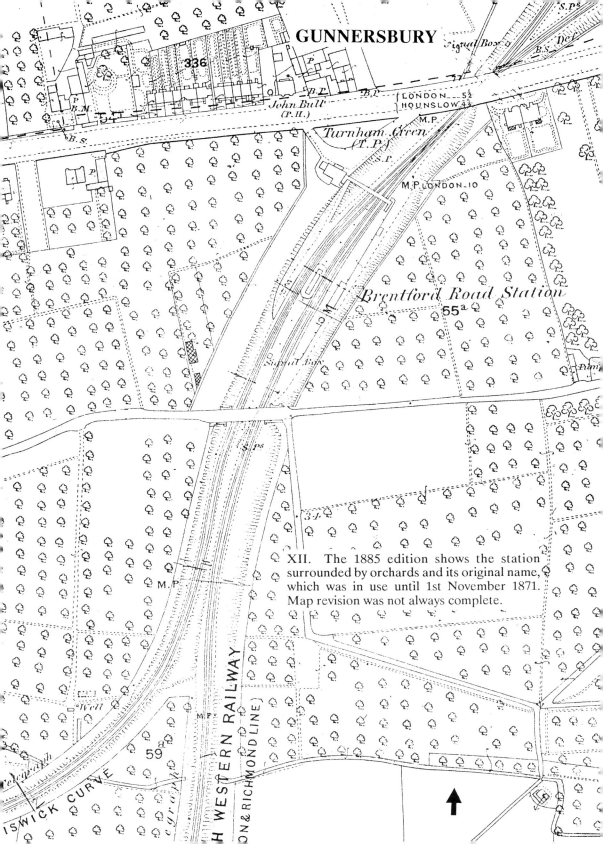

GUNNERSBURY

336

John Bull
(P.H.)

LONDON 52
HOUNSLOW

Turnham Green
(T.P.)

M.P. LONDON 10

Brentford Road Station
55ᵃ

Signal Box

34

XII. The 1885 edition shows the station surrounded by orchards and its original name, which was in use until 1st November 1871. Map revision was not always complete.

M.P.

59

CHISWICK CURVE

H WESTERN RAILWAY

ON & RICHMOND LINE

Well

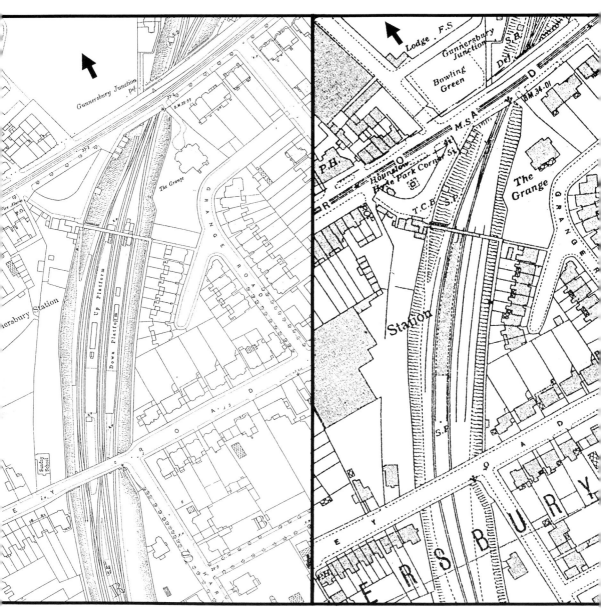

XIII. The 1894 edition reveals the extent of the two island platforms which enabled the station to become an important traffic centre with trains running in four directions. A fifth through road is shown on the west side, this being lost in 1930 along with the adjacent up loop and down main.

XIV. Closure of the Chiswick curve (lower left on map XII) and West Box (bottom of map XIII) took place on 24th July 1932. This simplified arrangement was effective from that day and is shown on the 1935 survey. The last train used the curve on 16th May 1932.

83. The station opened with the line on 1st January 1869 and was provided with a typical LSWR building of the period which survived until 1967. The maps show the J-shape approach road. (Lens of Sutton)

A 1992
(14) N. & S. W. J. RY.
Rail Motor Car Ticket.

Hammersm'h and Chiswick
Bath Road
Woodstock Road
Rugby Road
South Acton
Kew Bridge
Acton
Willesden

TURN OVER

1249
N. & S. W. June
Issued subject to the Company's Time Tables, Bills, and Notices.
Not transferable
HAMMERSMITH
TO
ACTON
First Class.

A 7751
(5) N. & S. W. J. RY.
Rail Motor Car Ticket.

Hammersm'h and Chiswick
Bath Road
Woodstock Road
Rugby Road
South Acton
Kew Bridge
Acton
Willesden

TURN OVER

84. Two island platforms and a fifth face on the left are evident. The two electrified lines were for Richmond services, the others connecting with the Chiswick curve. The latter was used by some long distance trains such as the Bradford - Portsmouth service from 1905 to 1908. A Manchester - Southampton train was routed this way from 1911. (Lens of Sutton)

86. The covered footbridge linked with the booking hall. Gas lights and the neglect caused by World War II and the subsequent period of austerity caused many suburban stations to appear drab. (Lens of Sutton)

85. North London Line trains stand at the one remaining island platform in about 1950. Note the length of the footbridge; it passes into the station building on the left and joins Grange Road on the right. (Lens of Sutton)

87. A vicious cyclone struck at 5.8pm on 8th December 1954 lifting the platform canopies, injuring several passengers and causing a trail of damage towards Willesden. The engine shed at South Acton (map VII) was destroyed. This is the scene next morning after the debris had been removed from the tracks and train services had been resumed. Linesmen are still at work. (J.C.Gillham)

88. The REC "South London Tour" passes through on the up line on 25th March 1962, headed by class O2 no. 30199. The route included the Shepperton branch, the H&C branch, Crystal Palace and Selhurst. (S.C.Nash)

89. Further clearance work was recorded on 7th March 1964 as preparations were being made to start work on office development. The nine-year old temporary roofing was still in place and a District Line "R" type train is in the up platform. (J.N.Faulkner)

90. Work was proceeding well on the major new development on 11th September 1964. A temporary footbridge was in place; no such exposed long bridge would be required in the new design. (J.C.Gillham)

91. A new bridge was built at the north end of the platforms. It was of much greater width and was recorded on the same day. A huge multi-storey office block would soon arise at the far end of the bridge. (J.C.Gillham)

→

92. It is clear that the temporary canopy supports were constructed from scaffolding. The window bars on the compartment stock were necessary on account of limited clearances in Hampstead Heath Tunnel. The trains were painted dark green at this period, having had at least seven different liveries since 1916. (J.C.Gillham)

→

93. A temporary ticket office was erected on the west side of the cutting; the access to the footbridge is on the left. Its successor was even less elegant. (J.C.Gillham)

94. This and the next two photographs were taken in the summer of 1985. The new flat roofed temporary-looking ticket office on the platform is in sharp contrast to the solid looking surroundings. A 2EPB unit departs with a window sticker - *Richmond*. (T.Wright)

95. Bearing a crooked sticker *North Woolwich*, an ageing 2EPB drifts down the 1 in 232 into the platform. The motor coaches of these units gave a particularly rough ride. (T.Wright)

96. The tidy exterior gave a good impression to potential rail travellers in September 1995. However, North London trains were only running as far as Willesden Junction owing to work in deepening Hampstead Heath Tunnel in connection with AC overhead electrification. The bulk of the building hides the entrance from the east along Chiswick High Road. (M.J.Stretton)

97. The redevelopment provided new offices for the computer firm, IBM. More recently they have been used by the British Standards Institute. Many might wish that they had a standard for new platform accommodation. The ticket "box" and the crossover were both still in situ in 1996. (T.Wright)

SOUTH OF GUNNERSBURY

98. An interesting southward view from Wellesley Road bridge shows the Richmond line climbing on the left and the Chiswick curve on the right. The curve and West Box (centre) were both closed on 29th May 1932. (Lens of Sutton)

99. Standing on the 1 in 100 gradient down from the bridge over the River Thames on 18th October 1981 is no. 33109 with an engineers train. The flats which stand on the site of the long-closed curve are euphemistically known as Chiswick Village. (R.Palmer)

100. Little wonder that the LSWR initially chose two reversals for the trains to Richmond in preference to a new river crossing. Two views from September 1995 reveal the magnitude of the construction task. (T.Wright)

101. The tidal Thames attracts a variety of
birds. The passage of a 313 unit over Strand
Green bridge does not disturb them. This is the
railway name; the district is correctly Strand-
on-the-Green. Very old and well preserved
luxurious dwellings border the towpath in the
foreground. (T.Wright)

KEW GARDENS

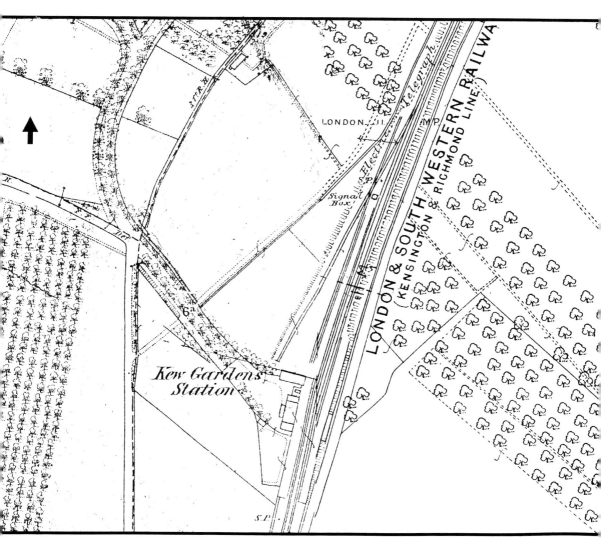

XV. The station was standing in splendid isolation in a rural setting when the 1886 survey was undertaken. One of the two sidings served an up bay platform in the early years. Both sidings were in use until 4th July 1931.

102. Rusty conductor rails suggest that this northward view was recorded just before electric services commenced on the District Railway in 1905. Note the differing signal posts. (Lens of Sutton)

103. An exceptionally wide up platform was provided to deal with the crowds returning from a visit to the nearby Royal Botanic Gardens. Upon arrival they had to use the subway, as the bridge over the platforms is devoted to a public footpath. This photograph is from 1953, as is the next one. (Pamlin Prints)

104. This northward view features the cross-over and the signal box, both of which were taken out of use on 31st January 1954, when automatic intermediate signals were introduced. (Pamlin Prints)

105. A 1963 photograph shows the similarity of the architecture to Gunnersbury, although many details differ. The gardens were originally those of a royal palace situated on the south bank of the Thames, the latter providing good transport to London in the pre-railway age. (Pamlin Prints)

106. Showing headcode B4 and a half yellow end, a class 501 accelerates away towards the last stop on its journey to Richmond. The view is from High Park Road bridge on 23rd May 1964. (T.Wright)

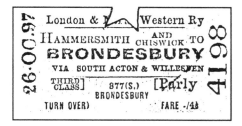

107. The station has a healthy day-long traffic which includes residents, botanists and historians; the Public Record office is a short walk to the north. The pleasant environs were recorded in September 1995. (M.Turvey)

108. Comparison of this 1995 view with the 1953 picture no. 103 shows how the old refreshment room has been cleaned and extended to meet the needs of the contemporary tourist. The "D" type District Line train is bound for Upminster. (M.J.Stretton)

109. Rounding the final curve in 1914 is a Waterloo to Richmond train. It has run via Kensington, Shepherds Bush, Hammersmith, Turnham Green and Gunnersbury. (D.Cullum coll.)

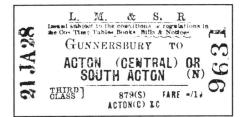

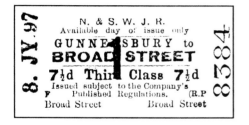

XVI. Richmond Gasworks was established in 1848 but the siding did not appear until 1882. It is an extension of the timber merchant's siding and was worked by horse. Coal consumption was 13000 tons in 1882, this later rising to 22400 tons in the peak year. The works ceased production in 1933 but a gas holder was still standing in 1996. The Waterloo-Richmond route runs from right to left and the line from Kew Gardens is at the top.

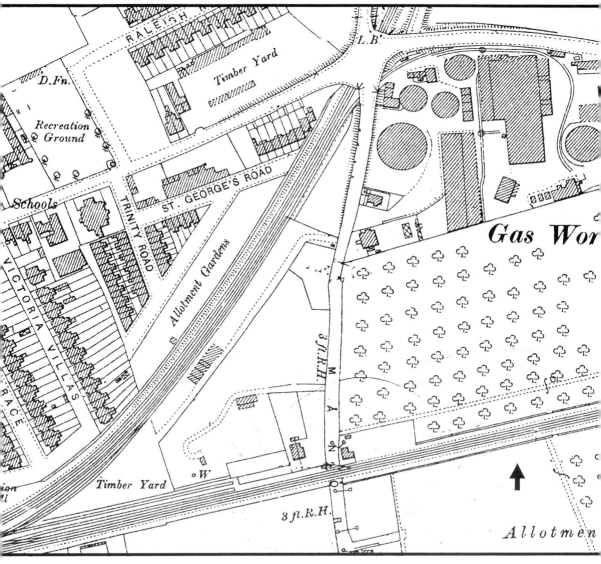

RICHMOND

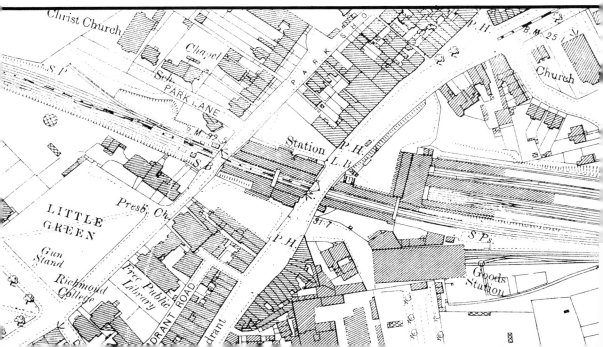

110. A 1953 panorama includes Oerlikon stock arriving from Broad Street and a 4SUB from Waterloo, the latter destined for the Hounslow Loop. Double gates are provided across the two sidings into Hazelby's timber yard. The right signal gave direct access to the Southern main line; the junction was taken out of use on 28th December 1972.
(Pamlin Prints)

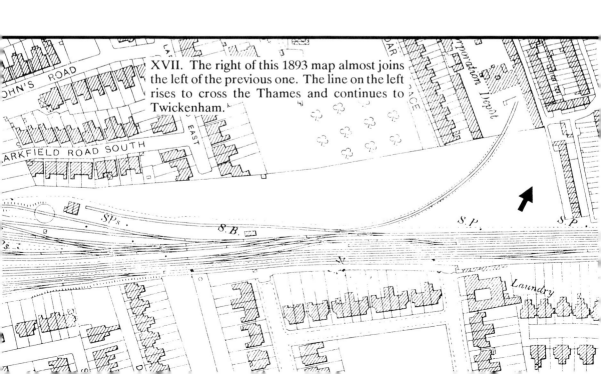

XVII. The right of this 1893 map almost joins the left of the previous one. The line on the left rises to cross the Thames and continues to Twickenham.

111. The 1869 terminus is on the right and the covered footbridge to the down platform is in the centre. Beyond are the roofs of the buildings of the main line station which opened on 22nd August 1848. On the left is the goods yard which was replaced by a new one on the up side in November 1936. The goods shed had acted as the terminus for two years from 27th July 1846. (Lens of Sutton)

112. Of interest in this view is a Metropolitan Railway train destined for Aldgate via Turnham Green and Paddington. Note the large condensing pipe for use on the underground part of the route east of Paddington. This photo was taken from Church Road bridge. (R.M.Casserley coll.)

113. Salmon pink and brown coaches of the LSWR are evident as a down train arrives from Waterloo on the direct line via Putney behind an 0-4-4T. (Lens of Sutton)

116. The five terminal platforms were little altered but their concourse was modernised in 1937. The SR style hexagonal lampshades were used throughout and electric lights replaced gas. In the early 1990s, most LT trains used platforms 6 and 7 (right), 4 and 5 being the domain of NL services. (Lens of Sutton)

117. A 1962 photograph reveals the fine tracery cast into the stanchion brackets, while the driver of a class 501 checks the rear of his train before returning to Broad Street. Compare with picture no. 114 to see that the middle siding has lost its conductor rails. The crossovers were removed in 1940 and the siding taken out of use in 1970. (Pamlin Prints)

118. A North London train arrives as a District Line C69 train departs on 10th November 1979. The connection to platform 3 in the centre foreground was taken out of use in November 1974 and the one on the right added for use by Southern Region parcel trains. The former was reinstated in 1985. The signal box replaced two on 28th January 1940 but controlled the Gunnersbury line only from 24th February 1980. (R.Palmer)

119. The reason for restoring the connection for North London trains to platform 3 is evident here on 17th June 1986. The 2EPB units were maintained at Selhurst Depot and so the link was used until October 1989 when the class 313 units were introduced. These trains being cared for at Bletchley. (J.N.Faulkner)

For other views and maps of this station, see the companion album *Waterloo to Windsor.*

120. The 1936 facade was photographed in 1995 when the entire area was under threat of complete redevelopment to provide a large number of retail units, formerly known as shops. A link with the past was made in 1985 with the transfer here of the NLR war memorial from Broad Street. (M.J.Stretton)

MP Middleton Press

Easebourne Lane, Midhurst. West Sussex. GU29 9AZ   Tel: 01730 813169   Fax: 01730 812601

. . . . . Write or telephone for our latest list . . . . .

BRANCH LINES
Branch Line to Allhallows
Branch Lines to Alton
Branch Lines around Ascot
Branch Line to Bude
Branch Lines around Canterbury
Branch Lines to East Grinstead
Branch Lines around Effingham Jn
Branch Lines to Exmouth
Branch Line to Fairford
Branch Line to Hawkhurst
Branch Lines to Horsham
Branch Lines around Huntingdon
Branch Lines to Ilfracombe
Branch Line to Lyme Regis
Branch Line to Lynton
Branch Lines around March
Branch Lines around Midhurst
Branch Lines to Newport
Branch Line to Padstow
Branch Lines around Portmadoc 1923-46
Branch Lines around Porthmadog 1954-94
Branch Lines to Seaton & Sidmouth
Branch Line to Selsey
Branch Lines around Sheerness
Branch Line to Southwold
Branch Line to Swanage
Branch Line to Tenterden
Branch Lines to Torrington
Branch Lines to Tunbridge Wells
Branch Line to Upwell
Branch Lines around Weymouth

LONDON SUBURBAN RAILWAYS
Caterham and Tattenham Corner
Clapham Jn. to Beckenham Jn.
Crystal Palace and Catford Loop
Holborn Viaduct to Lewisham
London Bridge to Addiscombe
Mitcham Junction Lines
South London Line
West Croydon to Epsom
Willesden Junction to Richmond
Wimbledon to Epsom

STEAMING THROUGH
Steaming through Cornwall
Steaming through East Sussex
Steaming through the Isle of Wight
Steaming through Surrey
Steaming through West Hants
Steaming through West Sussex

GREAT RAILWAY ERAS
Ashford from Steam to Eurostar
Festiniog in the Fifties

COUNTRY BOOKS
Brickmaking in Sussex
East Grinstead Then and Now

SOUTH COAST RAILWAYS
Ashford to Dover
Bournemouth to Weymouth
Brighton to Eastbourne
Brighton to Worthing
Chichester to Portsmouth
Dover to Ramsgate
Hastings to Ashford
Ryde to Ventnor
Worthing to Chichester

SOUTHERN MAIN LINES
Bromley South to Rochester
Charing Cross to Orpington
Crawley to Littlehampton
Dartford to Sittingbourne
East Croydon to Three Bridges
Epsom to Horsham
Exeter to Barnstaple
Exeter to Tavistock
Faversham to Dover
Haywards Heath to Seaford
London Bridge to East Croydon
Orpington to Tonbridge
Sittingbourne to Ramsgate
Swanley to Ashford
Three Bridges to Brighton
Tonbridge to Hastings
Victoria to Bromley South
Waterloo to Windsor
Woking to Southampton
Yeovil to Exeter

COUNTRY RAILWAY ROUTES
Andover to Southampton
Bath to Evercreech Junction
Bournemouth to Evercreech Jn
Burnham to Evercreech Junction
Croydon to East Grinstead
East Kent Light Railway
Fareham to Salisbury
Guildford to Redhill
Porthmadog to Blaenau
Reading to Basingstoke
Reading to Guildford
Redhill to Ashford
Salisbury to Westbury
Strood to Paddock Wood
Taunton to Barnstaple
Westbury to Bath
Woking to Alton

TROLLEYBUS CLASSICS
Croydon's Trolleybuses
Woolwich & Dartford Trolleybuses

TRAMWAY CLASSICS
Aldgate & Stepney Tramways
Bournemouth & Poole Tramways
Brighton's Tramways
Bristol's Tramways
Camberwell & W. Norwood Tramwa
Croydon's Tramways
Dover's Tramways
East Ham & West Ham Tramways
Embankment & Waterloo Tramway
Exeter & Taunton Tramways
Greenwich & Dartford Tramways
Hampstead & Highgate Tramways
Hastings Tramways
Ilford & Barking Tramways
Kingston & Wimbledon Tramways
Lewisham & Catford Tramways
Maidstone & Chatham Tramways
North Kent Tramways
Portsmouth's Tramways
Southampton Tramways
Southend-on-sea Tramways
Thanet's Tramways
Victoria & Lambeth Tramways
Walthamstow & Leyton Tramways
Wandsworth & Battersea Tramway

OTHER RAILWAY BOOKS
Garraway Father & Son
Industrial Railways of the South Eas
London Chatham & Dover Railway
South Eastern Railway
War on the Line

MILITARY BOOKS
Battle over Portsmouth
Battle Over Sussex 1940
Blitz Over Sussex 1941-42
Bognor at War
Bombers over Sussex 1943-45
Military Defence of West Sussex

WATERWAY ALBUMS
Hampshire Waterways
Kent and East Sussex Waterways
London to Portsmouth Waterway
West Sussex Waterways

BUS BOOK
Eastbourne Bus Story

SOUTHERN RAILWAY
● VIDEOS ●
Memories of the Hayling Island Bran
Memories of the Lyme Regis Branc
War on the Line